Diving

Tony Norman

INSIDE STORY

Copyright © ticktock Entertainment Ltd 2006
First published in Great Britain in 2006 by ticktock Media Ltd,
Unit 2, Orchard Business Centre, North Farm Road,
Tunbridge Wells, Kent TN2 3XF

ISBN 1 86007 850 8
Printed in China

Picture credits (t=top; b=bottom; c=centre; l=left; r=right): 20C Corbis; 29B: Lisa
Graham/Desert Divers www.desert-divers.com; 13 B: Fred Bavendam/Minden
Pictures/FLPA; 13 B: Frank W Lane/FLPA; 12BR: Colin Marshall/FLPA; 25 BL, B,
BR: 13 BR: D P Wilson/FLPA; 22B Norbert Wu/Minden Pictures/FLPA; 29 BR: The
Florida Tourist Board; 26 CR: NASA; 24C, 28 BR, 29 TTR, 29 TCR : NOAA; 8C
Montana Miller; 26 BR: Liz Baird/NOAA; 25BL, 26 TR: Ocean Explorer/NOAA; 27
B, BR: OAR/National Undersea Research Program (NURP); 6C: Red Bull (c)Stefan
Aufschnaiter; 9T Red Bull (c)Bernhard Spöttel; 5BL, 7T, 7CR: Red Bull (c)Mark
Watson; 25T: Gregory Ochocki/Science Photo Library; 4BL, 5BR, 5TCL, 5TR, 15T,
17T, 18C, 19T, 22C, 23T: Stockbyte; 11T, 12C: Yvonne Kamp, Whale Watch South
Africa; 10C, 13 T: Marion Ritter, White Shark Diving Company

The publishers would like to thank Desert Divers, The White Shark
Diving Company, Whale Watch South Africa and Red Bull for their help
in the making of this book.

Every effort has been made to trace the copyright holders, and we
apologise in advance for any unintentional omissions. We would be
pleased to insert the appropriate acknowledgements in any subsequent
edition of this publication.

Content

Introduction

There are more than 12 million divers in the world. They dive into a world of coral reefs, ice caves, underwater forests and blue holes. Divers also use deep water craft to go down over 11,000 metres (36,000 feet). Many strange creatures live in the depths.

CLIFFS AND CAGES

In Mexico, cliff divers jump from over 30 metres (100 feet) and hit the water at 95 kph (60 mph). In South Africa, cage divers throw a mixture of fish and blood into the sea. This draws great white sharks to a steel cage, where divers wait for a close-up view.

WITH ICE OR WITHOUT?

Ice divers cut holes in frozen lakes, or in the ice covering the oceans of the Arctic and Antarctic. They need special dive suits to stay warm in the waters below. Diving in the warm waters of Australia's Great Barrier Reef means going back in time. The coral was formed over 8000 years ago. Now it is home to many beautiful fish.

Divers can be suddenly surrounded by a school of colourful fish.

DIVING FACTS - DID YOU KNOW?

The ocean covers 70 per cent of the Earth's surface and holds 97 per cent of the Earth's water. Most sea water is 4°C (39°F), just above freezing.

CAGE DIVING

SCUBA DIVING

ICE DIVING

DEEP SEA DIVING

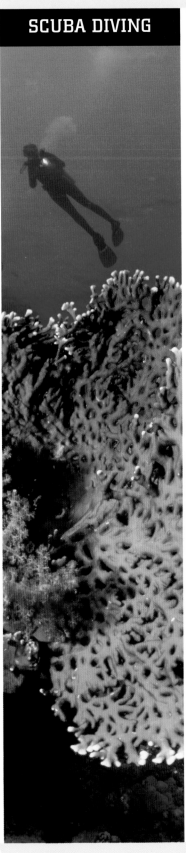

Beautiful sea dragons can be found around south and west Australia.

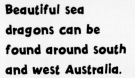

Divers often spot fish hiding from predators in coral or seaweed.

Cliff Diving

Cliff divers take off from heights of 25 to 35 metres (80-115 feet). Each dive lasts three seconds. The divers spin and twist in the air, then hit the water at over 100 kph (60 mph). Most divers land feet-first to reduce the risk of head and neck injury.

BRAVE HEARTS

The Hawaiian island of Lanai is where cliff diving first started. Warriors jumped from the cliffs to show their bravery. They used a rock ledge 26 metres (85 feet) above the sea. The same site is sometimes used for the World Cliff Diving Championships.

TOP HOT SPOT

Cliff divers in Acapulco, Mexico, give tourist shows every day. They must wait for high tide, when the water at the foot of the cliffs rises from 60cm to 365cm (2 feet to 12 feet).

Joey Zuber, one of the world's top cliff divers, in Kimberley, Western Australia.

Competition divers try to minimize the splash when they hit the water.

DIVING FACTS - DID YOU KNOW?

Cliff divers land in the water feet-first. If they hit seaweed or a fish, they are falling so fast they can break a foot, or even a leg.

Mazatlan, in west Mexico is a top spot for cliff divers.

TRUE STORIES

Wolfgangsee, Austria, 2005. Daniel Ballarin of the USA jumped off the 27 metre (88 feet) cliff and achieved the first-ever five-somersault dive in competition history.

Cliff divers jump into freshwater lakes as well as the sea.

Divers look for rocky outcrops above deep water.

No Place for Fear

Danger is part of cliff diving, but divers use their fear to make sure they are well prepared. Professional cliff divers always take care to plan ahead for the first dive of the day.

Dubrovnik in Croatia is growing in popularity for cliff divers.

THE DIVE ZONE

The 'Dive Zone' is the area of water where the divers must land. They check what is under the water to make sure there are no rocks or other dangers they need to know about. Then they do warm-up exercises for their legs, arms and backs, while focusing their minds on their first dive.

SHOW TIME

Every dive is a test of nerve and skill. One by one, the divers stand high on the cliffs. They look way down to the 'Dive Zone' where they will land. Then they rise up on their toes and dive out into thin air. They twist and spin before hitting the water feet-first. A diver is in the air for just three seconds before hitting the water.

Montana Miller was one of the first women to dive from the cliffs in Acapulco in Mexico.

DIVING FACTS - **DID YOU KNOW?**

How high do cliff divers go? The world's best divers jump from cliffs that are three times higher than the top diving board in the Olympics.

Diving into Ionian Sea on the Greek island of Corfu.

TRUE STORIES

Mexico 1976. America's Pat Sucher became the first American to win the Acapulco Cliff Diving Championships. He got the perfect score of 10 points in all five rounds.

Most injuries happen when a diver lands on their back or chest.

Cliff diving requires no specialist equipment.

Diving from the high cliffs of Acapulco in Mexico.

Cage Diving

The main thrill of cage diving is seeing great white sharks at close range. Divers watch the sharks through the bars of a steel cage. Cage diving is about seeing great whites swimming free in the ocean.

BEST DIVES

Cage diving trips are run by expert teams. Some of the best dive sites are in the ocean waters off South Africa, South Australia, Mexico and California.

Adult great white sharks are about 4-5 metres (13-19 feet) long.

BLOOD IN THE WATER

The crew of the cage diving boat throw an oily mushy mix of fish called 'chum' into the sea. Sharks are drawn by the smell of blood in the water. When the sharks appear, the divers climb into the cage, the lid is shut tight, and then the cage is lowered into the water. The cage, which is tied to the boat by strong nylon rope, floats a short distance from the boat, sometimes no more than 2-3 metres (6-9 feet).

A great white will usually eat fish, squid, other sharks, whales, dolphins and sea lions.

DIVING FACTS - DID YOU KNOW?

Great white sharks must swim constantly otherwise they will sink. They can smell a single drop of blood in 100 litres (26 gallons) of water.

Guns and spears are only used as a last resort.

TRUE STORIES

New Zealand, 2004. Four swimmers saw a great white in the sea. A group of dolphins swam round and kept them safe for 40 minutes, before the shark swam away.

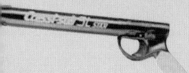

Chum is an oily mush of fish. Chum pellets are sometimes used.

Underwater cameras are a must. Most people want a record of the encounter.

Shark's Eyes

Most diving cages are small, but very strong. The bars can stand the fury of a shark attack, although these are rare. Divers wear wet suits, boots, gloves and a mask. They also wear a weight belt which helps them to stand and balance under water.

INSIDE THE CAGE

Divers must stay very still inside the diving cage. Great whites swim right up to the bars. Some people want to feel the skin of the shark, but this is strictly forbidden. The sharks are dangerous wild predators.

RIGHT OR WRONG?

Some people think cage diving is wrong. They say it encourages sharks to link humans to food and increases the number of attacks. Cage divers say there is no proof this is true. They say cage diving is a unique opportunity to get a close-up view of sharks.

Great white sharks have about 3000 teeth arranged in several rows.

The dorsal fin can be seen above the water when the shark is near the surface.

DIVING FACTS - DID YOU KNOW?

Only three species of shark are dangerous to humans, and there are less than 10 deaths a year from shark attacks. But every year humans kill 100 million sharks.

Many sharks are fairly small: the coral cat shark is only 60cm (2 feet) long.

TRUE STORIES

San Francisco 2002. Surfer Lee Fontan was on the beach when a shark jumped from the sea and bit him on the back and leg. Lee got free but he needed 100 stitches in his wounds.

With its eyes wide apart, the hammerhead shark has good vision.

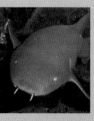

Nurse sharks live in groups in shallow waters.

Like most sharks, female smooth hounds are larger than males.

Scuba Diving

Divers that carry their own air supply with them are called scuba divers. The air comes from a cylinder on their back. In calm waters, the air lasts for about one hour.

FIRST LESSONS

Scuba diving lessons start from the age of 12. Learning how to scuba dive takes five or six lessons. Scuba divers learn how to put on a wet suit, mask and flippers, how to use the equipment and diving techniques.

Scuba divers wear large wide flippers that help them move through the water.

THE SARDINE RUN

One of the most spectacular scuba diving experiences is the Sardine Run. Every winter, millions of sardines swim up the coast of South Africa to find warmer waters, and thousands of scuba divers go to see them. There are so many fish they can be seen from the skies above. The Sardine Run is a feeding frenzy for dolphins, fur seals, whales and many kinds of shark. When the hunters move in on the fish, scuba divers get a close-up look as the sardines twist and turn like huge silver clouds under the sea.

A cylinder usually contains about 20 per cent oxygen, 80 per cent nitrogen – just like surface air.

DIVING FACTS – DID YOU KNOW?

Divers get a close up view of dolphin hunts during the Sardine Run. The dolphins force the shoals of fish into a shape like a ball, then close in and feast on the sardines.

Are you OK?

TRUE STORIES

Andrew Aitkin, a marine scientist, has studied the Sardine Run. "We don't really know why they do it," he said. "It is not a true migration as the sardines do not travel for feeding or breeding."

Stop

Out of air

Ears not clearing

Scuba's Mega Mix

Australia's Great Barrier Reef is one of the world's best scuba diving sites. It is made up of over 2000 small coral reefs. Other top coral reefs are those in the Caribbean, the Red Sea and Polynesia.

Coral reefs grow in clear, shallow, tropical waters.

IT'S A LIVING THING

The Great Barrier Reef is over 8000 years old and is so big that you can see it from space. It has over 1500 breeds of fish, 500 types of seaweed and 400 types of coral. Coral grows at about 1-2cm (1/2 inch) per year.

KELP FORESTS

Kelp is a type of seaweed. Kelp plants look like underwater trees. They grow up from the seabed and can be 40 metres (130 feet) tall. The kelp beds off the coast of California are home to sea otters, seals, snails, crabs and jellyfish. Great white sharks have also been seen there. Tasmania's kelp forests have whales, sea horses and huge rock lobsters.

Sea turtles spend most of their lives in water, only coming on land to lay their eggs.

DIVING FACTS – DID YOU KNOW?

Sea horses are the only animal in which the male becomes 'pregnant'. He gives birth to about 50 babies at one time.

Boat
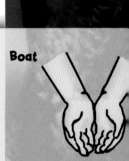

TRUE STORIES

Australia 1998. Two American scuba divers died in the shark-filled seas of the Great Barrier Reef. A tourist dive boat left them behind by mistake. Their bodies were never found.

...Me, or watch me

(Present) depth?

Buddy up

Blue Holes

Blue holes can be found in the Caribbean Sea and around the Bahamas. They were once caves on dry land, but the sea covered them thousands of years ago. The roofs of the caves fell in, leaving the blue holes we see today.

SECRETS OF THE DEEP

Dives into blue holes can last over an hour. Divers carry double air tanks and are linked together by safety ropes. They carry one main dive light and two back-up lights. Thicker wet suits than usual (7mm) may be worn to combat the cold water. Many deep cave divers also wear a computerised depth gauge and timer on their wrists.

BELIZE MYSTERY

The Great Blue Hole, near Belize, is one of the best dives in the world. The hole is 305 metres (1000 feet) wide and 125 metres (412 feet) deep. There are many tunnels in the Great Blue Hole. Divers have swum to the end of many, but some have never been fully explored.

Many fish living in deep-water caves have no fear of people.

DIVING FACTS - DID YOU KNOW?

The Great Blue Hole is known as one of the world's best shark dives. The shark species include hammerheads, bulls, lemons, black tips and tiger sharks.

Cave divers must always go in pairs, never alone.

It is dark and dangerous, but cave divers explore a world very few other people will ever see.

TRUE STORIES

In the Bahamas, local legends tell of the lusca who live in the blue holes. These evil creatures are half-dragon, half-squid, and they pull swimmers deep underwater to their deaths.

Many unique plants and animals live in the deepest caves.

Light shows cave divers the way back to the exit.

Ice Diving

Divers must take great care to stay warm. Drysuits have a seal at the neck and wrists to keep out the icy water. Underneath, the divers wear a special undersuit to protect them from the cold. Divers also wear hoods, gloves and full face masks.

HARD TRUTH

Divers use a pick axe or chain saw to cut a hole in the ice. They drop down through the hole into the water. Ice diving is dangerous. Divers are tied to a rope. Divers use rope signals so they can be pulled up to the surface if they are in trouble. A rescue diver waits, ready to enter the water if the first diver is in trouble. Ice dives only last about 20 minutes, because of the icy cold water.

ICE CAVES

Under the ice, the sea glows in shades of blue and green. There are tunnels through the ice. Ice caves are beautiful. Their walls look like glass.

Most ice diving takes place in frozen lakes, although some divers brave icy seas.

Studying the ice at the Antarctic and Arctic can help scientific research.

DIVING FACTS - DID YOU KNOW?

Ice divers in Canada's Arctic Bay have a good chance of seeing polar bears. There are about 30,000 polar bears left in the world. Half of them live in Canada.

Ice picks are carried to break through the ice.

TRUE STORIES

North Pole, April 1999. Bob Wass (USA), Michael Wolff (Austria) and Brett Cormick (UK) became the first team to dive under the ice at the North Pole. All three came home safe and well.

Scuba divers wear special drysuits to keep warm.

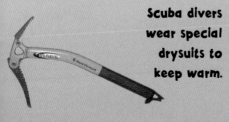

Gloves must be thick and warm with a good grip.

The light is dim under the ice. So torches are a must.

Deep Sea Diving

Most scuba diving takes place in shallow water close to land. But 90 per cent of the sea is over one kilometre deep. The deepest part of the Pacific Ocean is 11,033 metres (36,200 feet). There are huge areas of the seabed we know nothing about. Deep sea divers plan to change that.

Professional divers are sometimes employed to explore wrecks in the deep ocean.

DEEP SEA DANGER

Deep sea divers wear an all-steel suit and a metal helmet, worn with heavy lead boots. Divers have a line that links them to the boat above. The line supplies air, power for underwater lighting and a link to the surface at all times.

SPACE AGE DIVES

Jim Suits look like a space suit, with big bendy arms and metal hands. A clear dome covers the head. Power boosters help divers 'jump' under the sea. The suits weigh 450 kg (1000lb) and have their own air supply. They make it possible for divers to go down to depths of almost 600 metres (2000 feet).

The spotted ratfish lives in cold water at depths up to 900 metres (2,900 feet).

DIVING FACTS - DID YOU KNOW?

Divers who come up too fast from a deep dive can get the bends (decompression sickness), which can cause body pains, dizzy spells and sickness.

Thermal diving under suit worn under a drysuit.

TRUE STORIES

The deepest human dive ever was in the Mariana Trench near Japan in 1960. Two men in the deep sea sub The Trieste went down to 10,915 metres (over 35,000 feet). This record may never be broken.

Fully breathable, watertight drysuit with reinforced knees and seat.

A tough, comfortable drysuit specially designed for women divers.

A waterproof wristwatch will show divers how long they have been underwater.

Monsters of the Deep

No light shines in the deepest parts of the ocean. Strange fish swim in the dark waters. They have been there for millions of years. It is a world we know very little about.

WEIRD WORLD

Giant squid can grow up to 20 metres (65 feet) long. They use the big suckers on their ten legs to catch and hold their prey. Then they use their sharp beaks for the kill. Vampire squid live as deep as 900 metres (3000 feet) and have a light-producing organ in their body they can turn on and off. They have sharp spikes and look like something out of a space movie!

INTO THE FUTURE

The United States will launch a new deep sea sub in 2008. It will be able to dive down to over 99 per cent of the world's seabed, hitting depths of over 6,500 metres (21,000 feet).

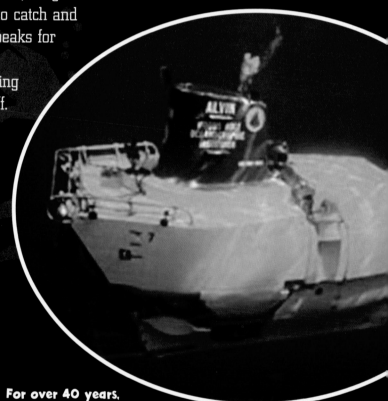

For over 40 years, scientists have explored the ocean depths in the submersible Alvin.

DIVING FACTS - DID YOU KNOW?

Deep water hagfish dig into the flesh of other fish, them eat them alive from the inside out.

The black sea dragon has a fishing lure in front of its mouth to attract prey.

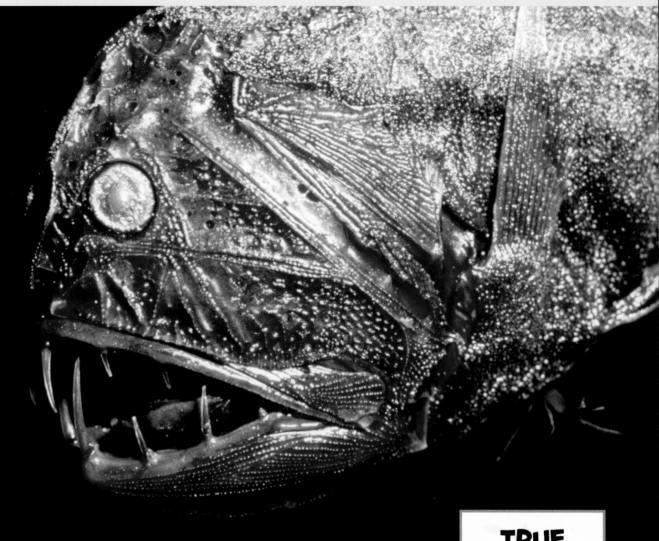

The fangtooth has a short body, large head and long teeth. Luckily it is only 15cm (6 in) long.

TRUE STORIES

Sperm whales like to hunt giant squid. The whales take a big breath then dive deep to catch their prey. The whales can stay underwater for up to an hour.

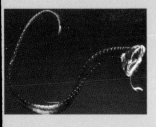

The deep sea anglerfish has a bioluminescent light at the end of its 'pole'.

The deep sea gulper has a hinged mouth that can swing wide open for large prey.

Brave Hearts

When the warriors of Hawaii jumped from the cliffs into the sea, thousands of years ago, they did it to show they were not afraid. Courage has always been part of diving. Here are some more brave hearts...

The hardsuit allows divers to work in water up to 305 metres (1000 feet) deep.

HOUSE UNDER THE SEA

The American Sylvia Earle lived under the sea for two weeks in 1970 to study sea habitats, and the effects of living underwater on humans. Sylvia and her all-woman team could swim in and out of their 'home', which was in 15 metres (50 feet) of water. In 1979, Sylvia set a world record for the deepest solo dive: 381 metres (1,250 feet).

Deep sea subs are carefully monitored from the boat.

The Titanic, as it is today.

SIMPLY THE BEST

France's Jacques-Yves Cousteau helped make the first-ever scuba diving air tank. He called it an aqua-lung. Jacques loved the sea and made TV shows of his diving trips. He is the most famous diver of them all.

Jacques-Yves Cousteau gives a talk on his deep sea missions.

For some people, diving is a job as well as a hobby.

DIVING FACTS - DID YOU KNOW?

Robert Ballard has been on over 65 missions in deep-dive subs. He is the man who found the wreck of the Titanic in 1985.

TRUE STORIES

France 2004. Loic Leferme set the 'free diving' world record. He had no air tanks. He took one big breath and dived 171 metres (560 feet). The dive took 3 minutes 40 seconds.

Professional divers include scientists, and those working on pipes, oil rigs, ships and dams.

Sylvia Earle shows a colleague a shell.

Preparing to dive in a JIM suit.

Map of the Oceans

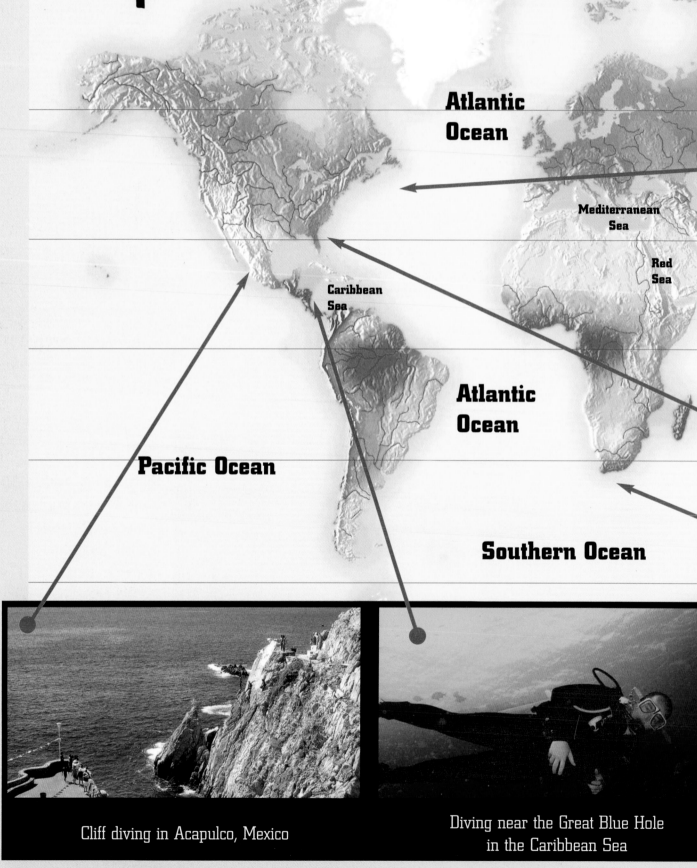

Atlantic
Ocean

Mediterranean
Sea

Red
Sea

Caribbean
Sea

Atlantic
Ocean

Pacific Ocean

Southern Ocean

Cliff diving in Acapulco, Mexico

Diving near the Great Blue Hole
in the Caribbean Sea

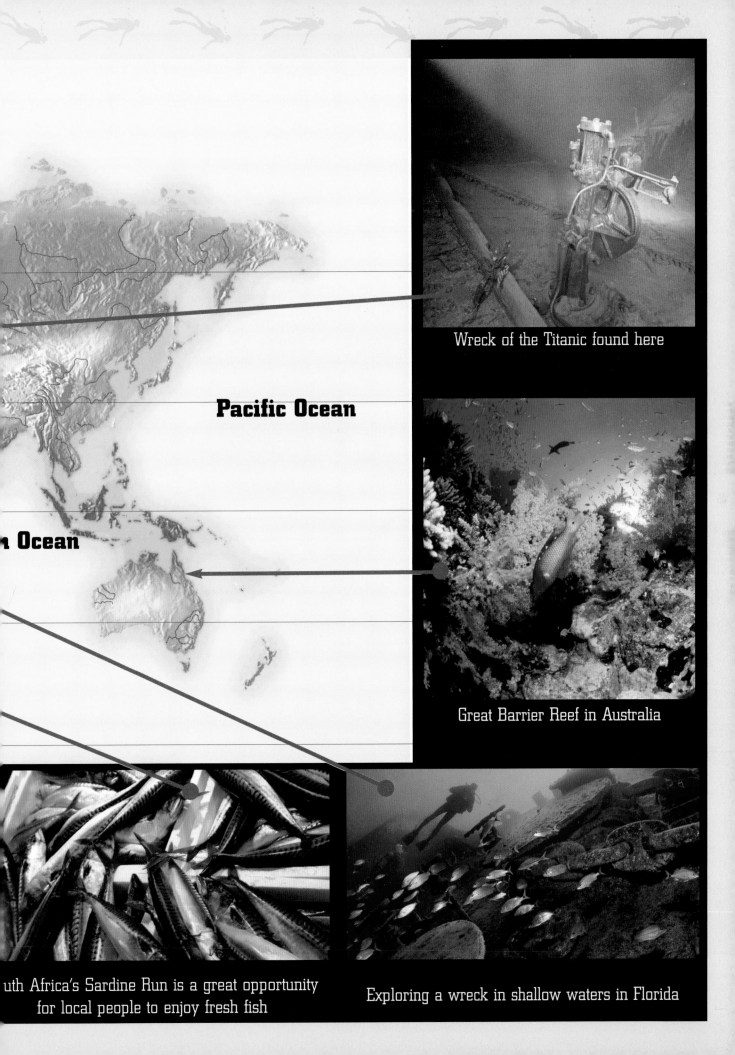

Pacific Ocean

Ocean

Wreck of the Titanic found here

Great Barrier Reef in Australia

uth Africa's Sardine Run is a great opportunity
for local people to enjoy fresh fish

Exploring a wreck in shallow waters in Florida

Glossary

Aqua-lung
A type of cylinder and regulator to allow divers to breathe under water

Bioluminescence
A light produced from living things

Blue holes
Underwater cave without a roof

Chum
Fishy mixture thrown into the sea to attract sharks and other fish

Coral
The skeletons of tiny marine animals called polyps that have formed rock-like deposits over thousands of years

Coral reef
Large area of coral, home to many species of fish

Cylinder
The tank used to store the air that they breathe under water

Depth guage
An instrument that tells divers how far under the water they are

Dive zone
The area of water a cliff diver aims to land in

Dorsal fin
The fin on a fish's back

Drysuit
A suit that traps a layer of air against the skin to keep a diver warm in cold water

Flippers
A flat rubber 'shoe' that helps divers power themselves through the water

Freshwater
Water that is not salty (ie, not seawater)

Free diving
Diving for as deep or as long as possible without the aid of breathing equipment

Great white
Type of large shark found in all oceans

Hardsuit
A metal suit used by deep sea divers

Jim suit
A reinforced diving suit that protects the diver from the water pressure during deep sea diving

Kelp
A type of large, brown seaweed

Migration
When animals travel to a different place in order to feed or breed

Predator
An animal that catches and eats other animal

Tank
Another word for the cylinder of air divers use under the water

Submersible (sometimes shortened to sub)
An underwater craft

Tether
A line linking the diver to the surface for safety

Titanic
A ship that hit an iceburg and sank in 1912

Undersuit
A layer of clothing (often thermal) worn under a drysuit for extra warmth

Warm-up
A series of stretches before exercise that help prevent injury to muscles

Wet suit
A tight fitting suit that traps a layer of water against the skin to keep a diver warm in water

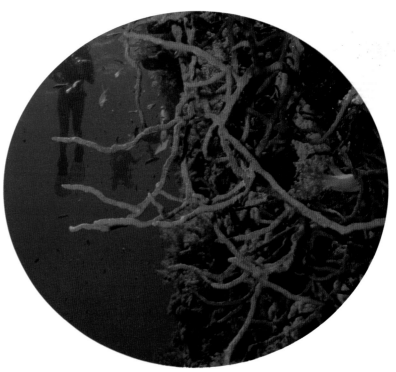

Index